a r d o r

a r d o r

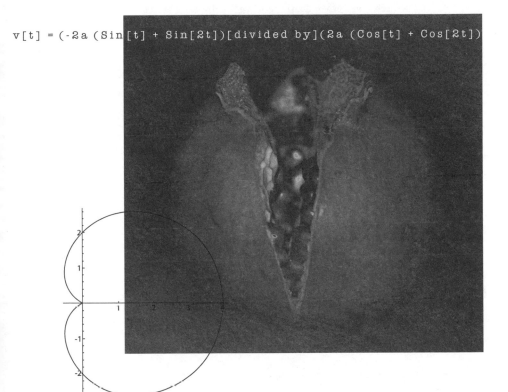

$$v[t] = (-2a\,(Sin[t] + Sin[2t])[divided\ by](2a\,(Cos[t] + Cos[2t])$$

karen an-hwei lee

T|P TUPELO PRESS

Grateful acknowledgment is made to *Puerto del Sol,* *New Orleans Review,* and *Columbia Poetry Review* where portions of this book first appeared.

Ardor
Copyright © 2008 Karen An-hwei Lee

ISBN 978-1-932195-69-9
Printed in the USA on an FSC certified paper

First paperback edition: October 2008
Library of Congress Control Number: 2008926701

Tupelo Press
Post Office Box 539, Dorset, Vermont 05251
(802) 366-8185
www.tupelopress.org

Tupelo Press is an award-winning independent literary press that publishes fine fiction, non-fiction and poetry in books that are as much a joy to hold as they are to read. Tupelo Press is a registered 501(c)3 non-profit organization and relies on donations to carry out its mission of publishing extraordinary work that may be outside the realm of the large commercial publisher.

Cover photograph by Shigeru Tanaka, amana images collection, Copyright © Getty Images, Inc.

contents

The word is near you;
it is in your mouth and in your heart.

ROMANS 10:8

Faith is that quality or power
by which the things desired
become the things possessed.

KATHRYN KUHLMAN

It is hard to describe
a luminous window of sparse moonlight,
translucent shadows flowing in the wind.

LI QINGZHAO

ardor

. . .

Calque alphabet

Modulation with avian equivalence of hands

Translation perched around a white rose

Photographic grapheme of cardioid delight

Water potential, a hidden sonnet whose

Permissible boundary of closed form

Is a sequence or open cycle in

A heart-shaped curve traced by a point

On the circumference of a circle rolling

Around an equal fixed circle, general equation

$\rho = a(1 + \cos\theta)$ *in polar coordinates*

As a child I knew how to sketch this

Graph a cardioid around plotted

Birds from real algebraic equations

Conversation images of empirical scent

I slipped this dream out of its own skin

Put its shape inside a bottle, this one

Joined its hands to prayer, this one

Jin wei first tone fourth tone

Merged rivers of contrasting hues

One opaque, the other clear

. . .

dream   Hunger not as the absence of what is desired, rather, its own presence, thirst without conditional reciprocity. Raised on unconditional love. Sustenance in shape of beggar's poultry, blackened tea leaves wrapped inside a thin bread caul, the whole bird roasted in a clay pot over an open fire. Once made for the working now also served to the wealthy. Will the bird rise flaming out of broken light? The blind woman asks, does a burning bird secrete any more tears when desired?

. . .

Men better be careful when they fall in love with her

Looks like a shallow forest since she appears so young

Thin shoulders sparsely envoiced of birdlight

Shafts falling through fern and pine

Light moss and a new path in the afternoon, not wild

Song cycle hiding a water sonnet

The men go a little ways in

Fall off a cliff

. . .

Coating of time

the color of patina

resembles sherry or amaretto

after putting on a light dress. Lightness:

she wears a corsage to cover the remains.

The flow of blood widens through the heart

as water emerges from a narrow channel;

the flow of blood widens through the heart.

She wears a corsage to cover the remains

after putting on a light dress. Lightness

resembles sherry or amaretto

the color of patina,

coating of time.

. . .

He turned ten shades of beet red.

Why didn't he intercept the letter?

They took the pomegranate and burned it.

You mean they burst it open. Ripe.

Tore it apart leaf by leaf and burned the seeds.

Every single word in there said love and love.

Notebook of pomegranate seeds, that is.

Yes. Leaves all pinned together like children.

And burned the seeds, but that's all right.

For some, burning stimulates germination.

We shared fresh tea, the fire of life.

Don't know whether true for pomegranates.

They just need to see a little more light.

Seeds or violent cohorts?

Both need to see more.

. . .

Remember that time we went to the little bistro.

We weren't properly dressed. Paper bags.

But they let us in. It was the south side.

It was and that was all right.

How the woman sat at the table behind you.

Across from us. Alone at first, then a friend.

A gold-digger. You could tell by the conversation.

The woman advised us to try the tangerine quail.

I come here every night, she said. It's delicious.

Try the red wine when we heard plum.

We desired riesling, I remember.

She'd had a stroke, you surmised.

The way she phrased her words, tangerine.

Now the post office is closed on Sundays.

So much has changed since then.

I walk three miles now to mail a letter.

. . .

What marriage is, she says

You've never been married before

Tenderness of your left ventricle

Wedded to five fingers of love's opening

Laying a slip of flesh on the inside, outside

Five fingers of light, four-chambered heart

Lifted here and turned outward, a letter

Spoken aorta in the morning, no accident

Bottle of aspirins inside a fever, thinning blood

One's ear pressed to your turning auricle, rotating

Rotary tenderness of the aorta, glistening under

Green meadows, arched meadows, red besotted

Uncovering humble ardor servicing the orchard

Praying deep, this swimming briefcase of a body

Opened in silence, modest small of one's hidden back

Smaller than your nape, even your closed hand

Say not I but one not to eclipse the beloved

Whose body is slender as a cradle, one candle

Stirring the end of one's slumber, longevity

Is love alluvial, is this velocity, this hour

Called the shallows of eternity, I lay myself down

In your shallows, river whose eyes are pupiled dark

Intimate as the date-seller's, as the dates themselves

As young as the date-selling widow with bare hands

Pressing this red envelope of rooted adoration

Red dress with fish bones painted helter skelter

Opening there, your sight not keen enough

Rayed self lays herself down in your red shallows

After following you in rain the day before

Whole heart like a stone persimmon excavated

From a visceral mattress exchanged for

This one of flesh rights

Pronunciation of adze, pararosaniline

What is a paper wedding then

. . .

letter   About her second marriage, a potential forgery.

. . .

dream   A man with a ladder in the yard was picking lemons. Stealing lemons. He was seeing another man's wife, a married woman in his own backyard. The other man's that is. The one who owned the lemon tree. Looking at another woman's photograph, her soft gray silk. Hair. Iron candelabra near the autumn ladder.

. . .

Illness departs from your body, muslin lifted

Illness looks like muslin doesn't it

When it's not glaucoma, a film

For instance your affection is left to breathe

Pressure on the nerve not a cataract

You can read to the seventh line of the eye chart

Noticed that yesterday at the ophthalmologist's

Pressing the fragrance out of ordinary things

Essences, the meninges of happiness

Shunning places that resemble airports

Immigrant's vigilance and wariness

Transience and surface, certain trauma

Angels throwing down broken glass for safety

In front of the fire hydrant, no cars

Yesterday no one would park there

It was a blessing so I could rest

Immaculate mineral water

Only angels could afford such purity

Quality too, such resonant glass

I saw it with my own eyes

Breaking and shining, effulgent

Broken effulgence

No sadness

. . .

dream   A pomegranate tree same age as I am and in the same language. Nature of the language is not explained. The pomegranates are pale beige tinged with green, blush of pink, unripe and growing upward, soft as a child's hand with transparent hair like downy white peaches touched with equinoctial green. The pomegranate tree is not savage. It is a child.

dream   Yielding her body to prayer, lowering herself into a pool.

dream   The books grow wings for their destinations. Where? Palm springs? The desert? Chardonnay is left in the day room, direct sun. Pressed fruit ferments in darkness, attains the clarity of cologne. A tincture of violet dye so it doesn't resemble pure gin, though tinting fades with time.

dream We're not finished yet. Oranges. Still time to arrive at
the orchard.

. . .

Fascicle like fabulous and bicycle

Translated into a flock of birds

Unmerited favor

One iron-colored rose

I saw your hand lifted in a dream

I was praying for you

A sleeve of hot oil

Sclera edge of eye

Viscera bright as sealing wax

In the very mouth of the chofar

Last hour to enter with a shout

Not in part, but in whole

We shall know then

The sequential rose in whole

Petal on petal, bicycles

Dancing in loosed tongues

Paradise is an actual place

A finite number of cubits high

Slipped this dream

Out of its own skin

. . .

dream   Blue jays with hummingbird's wings hovering by the lake. Incarnations of a sad heart. Hybrid blue. Whose heart and why so blue remain questions. How, despite the weight of sadness, the jays hover without falling into the lake.

. . .

A man who desired to make love

Desired to hear the sound of tearing silk

Emerald silk and watered silk, old sienna

Women lined up on the street

No matter the original dye, indigo

Nervous quality of love

Tearing open error

This man, drinking heavily, dark and wilted

Orange lately salmon-colored, falling

Curled lilies parched and falling

Who is coming? asked one of the women

Lining the street for poultry sales

Didn't observe which way he turned

She and the others never looked back

High spirits waned as our boat turned late

Through a dense patch of fragrant lotus

Oaring and oaring, rowing . . . .

. . .

dream   The whole alley dug out like a grave, and the woman called all-of-the-above lay in bedroom darkness, gas and electricity off. Her daughter, still a child, was with child, and the blind woman saw the unborn's woes turning over, touching chin, eyes closed like twin resinous hips, beeswax rose knees in night water. I hoped he would marry me, said the girl with child, her eyes new jasmines. Meaning a grown white man.

...

Talking about a poet, a woman

What happened to her fascicles

Four hundred of them in the drawers

Underneath the bed, I remember

Or am I imagining this

Black spice cake

Hand-twisted rope

Lowered into the garden

From her upstairs window

Loved a young man who died

Consumption or fever something

Had other suitors, loved others

Including married men

One who moved to the other coast

Around here, as a matter of fact

Then, though, it was like relocating

All the way to the south pole or Asia

Why she spent all day in her room writing

Unscrolling handwritten dashes

A mustard-colored room

It's what I would rather do

Close the door when the suitors come

With their briefcases of paper

Don't standardize my phrasing

My seasoned grammar

Of double roses

Dashed rhododendrons

. . .

dream   A boat is built upside down, says the blind woman, for the sake of rainproofing and sealing the wood. It's simpler to build that way. I read about fishermen on micronesian archipelagoes whose boats are overturned. Slatted bleached bones, equatorial light shot through, almost verbalized emotion. Language of literal heat.

letter   In a dream, the word archipelago was algebra.

dream   A woman pulled on the corner of the table cloth and exposed a fish tank. Aquarium full of long-finned colored fish, long as her hands, turquoise, amethyst, green, yellow, emerald, gold, scarlet. The blind woman knew, then, this woman was concealing a pregnancy. Fish meant life. Colors meant progeny.

. . .

At midnight, we made love atop a steeple

Our bodies, turning still, did not rest

Stars emerged nightly through our bodies

Flesh pierced with cosmic dust

I took this journey alone

Horseradish manes blessing the wind

Why the words *ai* and *ai*

In this language

Are love and moxa

Nothing else is mentioned

About moxa wine

Our bodies shot through, stellar

Horseradish manes

Novel to this universe

. . .

Sleeping with freeway maps

Red arteries and boulevards

Mingling with future routes

Miracle of bilocation or image

Of the real in more than one place

Here and there like Christ

Coincident or incidental light

Appearing to the disciples

All this done without mirrors

Quoting oneself in terms

Eclipse of self and spirit

Remember the cross

Merited flame

Elliptical rose

Unwrapped

Insurmountable

Signature redolence free

Invisible ardor of devotion

One hand apart

. . .

dream   Even the deaf speak aloud in unknown tongues. No one can say it's imitation. Flames descend upon their heads. Glossolalia. Eyes closed. Uttering languages none has heard.

. . .

Inheritance

Prayer to release healing

To her body's collected remembrance

Of the indelible rose, diaspora

Smaller parts

Optic nerve, sclera

A word, indolence

Juxtaposed

To the word, grace

Not merely pooling

Intercession

Must engulf

Ignite

Flesh burning flesh

Vision joined to

Love's apostrophe

Of possession

. . .

dream   The blind woman, turning in her sleep miles north,
leans over my dream to see whether I am awake. I,
too, am sleeping and lean over her dream, sheltering
her. We are one another's present skin. Present kin,
she says. Your blood is my blood. Your blood is from
Asia as mine eons ago when everything was internally
bridged, one aortic root. One mitochondrial missus,
original woman.

prayer   Pierced outline of this woman's body, either one,
woman or woman.

dream   Inside is the careful verbal rose opening multifoliate
praise. Etched paradise is a walled city, walled garden
one hundred forty-four cubits high. Ardor is a
dispersed sequence of praise. Rises in direct relation,
utterance redolent with love. Forest outside is a young
universe but not shallow. Peeling sycamores, paper
birches. Sparse phrases equinoctial green within.

. . .

dream	Men go inside, fall off a cliff.
prayer	A cardioid, robust at one end to a point.
dream	What to do about these nervous, broken men?
prayer	Translated version of the algebraic heart.
letter	Flock of birds. Translingual migration.
letter	*Shing. Xing.* Transliterations of the heart.

. . .

Strong as my thigh with gold eyes and hunger.

What was it you saw this morning?

Red-tailed hawk under the old conifer.

You invaded his or her dining space.

Form of domestic space for a bird, wilderness.

Standing on a blue mourning dove, wings askew.

Leviticus lists all the unclean birds one must not eat.

Cuckoo in one translation, herring gull in another.

Hoopoe, great owl and little owl, the red kite.

Bird like the hawk or the kestrel. Ossifrage.

Breaker of bones such as the gier eagle.

Mourning doves make love in a pine's shadow.

Tremble on a rail, hooked into one another.

Tilting aeroplane outspread, dipping, yawing.

Calque alphabet of wing attached to keel.

Space of a colon, equivalence of avian epistrophe.

Above the colon, a bird's crop of pebbles.

Not a form of rhetorical address.

Without apostrophes, they never fail.

Unaware they live in time, molting.

Shedding their own manner of being.

. . .

dream   The blind woman goes upstairs to close the window, leaving only enough space for a rufous hummingbird or a drone. Why am I closing this window, says the blind woman. It's going to rain, that's why. November is the month of rains with premonitions.

prayer   Hover in still air by tracing infinity signs in parenthesis.

. . .

It's light shining over the flood

Before and after the breaking of the levee

Light the color of insulin, pale liquid intensity

Blood substance unlocked to sweet

Sky is the color of discarded cans

Mardi gras beads less iridescent in graphite mud

Actually the ocean melting inside the river inside

A house where the women's knitting circle met

Cadavers are tied to railings, not to drift away

In one cadaver's mouth, the blossom of ardor

24

In form of a bougainvillea petal, marking

The grace of this body apart from others

Three nights in a row during November

She dreamed of weddings, her body in a linen

Wedding dress impermeable as sailcloth, heavy

As though she would arrive at this point, then be still

A photograph of sound, sonogram of hand-trimmed

Bird's voices carrying seed pearls one by one to women

Working in the fields, rice sown to praise

The water roots of pure glass, industrial cadmium

Soluble in bone, water, and blood

. . .

dream   There was no groom, just an iceberg staircase and
broken glass in her hand more sea than cullet.
Brokenness did not hurt. Neither did absence. More
like soft cubes of bitter melon her mother used to
buy when she was a child, green and preserved sweet,
crystallized. New snow for the low ocean in her mouth
didn't burn, either. Wasn't new sea cullet washed
ashore with pointed faces. Facets. Each one is different,
her mother would say, putting the bitter melon in her
mouth, sweet. Each one is not bitter. Unique.

prayer   Surviving fragment of a letter inside the blind
woman's cabinet.

letter   To whom it may concern. This letter formally with-
draws the original poem entitled prayer II, since
archivists discovered prayer II and prayer III are

25

one and the same. When the latter was found, it was assumed that, since the former was II, the other must be III or I. II and III, however, are copies of one poem. Please note that a third poem may exist as prayer I or simply prayer.

dream   All prayers ever prayed, I, II, III, and so on, exist unnumbered. Original love with a watermark, a hinged infinity sign.

. . .

Two dark red lobes

Inside the bird

Issue hormones for spring

And possibly migration

Anything to do with growth

Molting

In all its forms, ardor

A rare being, rare find

Possible the bird

Spends days searching for

The most beautiful women

A history of them, eiderdowned

Fragrant in small groups and friendships

Remembering details and images fondly

Without shame, malt vinegar

Emotion

. . .

letter   Of an epilogue to records on metal and stone. *A man offered to sell us a painting of peonies by Xu Xi for the price of two hundred thousand copper coins. Even the wealthy couldn't afford it, but we took the scroll home to admire for a couple nights. After returning it to the seller, we faced one another, husband and wife, in profound sadness.*

. . .

The word, diurnal

Ink says, the present consists of

Floating diaries in blocks of prose

Pages numbered in parenthesis, yet by the time

Prose is written, it too is memory

The original deluge happened so long ago

It's an abstraction like anger or hunger

Through the breakage of bending ferns

Not a form of careless bricolage

Exposed fossils show signs of a global flood

Sudden rising waters, petrified form of tears

Books . . . a commissioned string of connected boats

Water evidenced in stone inscribed

A third of the bathroom tiles underwater

You lift them out by hand, one and one

Spare celadon separated floating on the sea

You want to see the color inside an avocado

One that you miss especially since

It's the color of ardor, the lightest part

Where you peel it away, almost pear

Green before this yellow contingency

Sort of green, sort of beige, in parenthesis

. . .

dream   What language the word, rood, is, and whether a transliteration or not.

prayer   All the languages she speaks flame into tongues, multifoliate, imbricated, inundated.

dream   Of the rood as an instrument of sacrifice regardless of alphabet.

letter   Regardless of lettering.

. . .

In November

The winter phase, solstice

Encampments are burning

A woman sets herself on fire

Survives with third-degree burns

Four different shootings this week

Eight people died

A woman who passed away

Returned with her mouth sewn shut

Crushed azalea inside her lips

Where her tongue had been

28

Hair was dark as horses, not light

As it was when she was alive

She was speaking to a man who

Soon too would be under the earth

The blind woman hears her say

Most painful is the mortician's sewing

The mouth closed, stitched shut

Before he did so, however, placed

The fragile azalea inside to sing

Under dark weight, soon crushed

Later that night, the blind woman

Sees this woman cutting a man's hair,

Wet on wet with a wet black comb

Her ironic possessions

In the string of boats

Ferrying books across a yellow river

After the tatars set fire to everything

How does a Song dynasty poet's

Collection of antiquities

Relate to me in this age

A heart-shaped curve traced by a point

The blind woman drinks quarts

Two mayonnaise jars of water

Around an equal fixed circle

She is not the burning woman

Breaking open the uncrushed world

Tears of myrrh

Of a single red atom ruptured

Hold on, says the blind woman

I must turn out the light

I am fasting now

On diluted honey

Remember this eye's

Circumference

In song

. . .

dream   Blue raspberries. Blue chemises.

dream   Women on completely different wavelengths.

dream   A young woman, not yet thirty, leaves a bowl of cooked lentils uncovered.

prayer   White vinegar as an antidote.

. . .

Blind woman's visual field

Where water turns coral violet with stone

As it does the farther out you swim

This shallow forest, young

Washing up black sea nettles

Fish bells resembling shower caps

Droves by the thousands, stinging

Ardor frilled and silent, soft-bodied

Swimmers must carry white vinegar

Pouring forth transparent antidote

Neutralize the transparent sting

. . .

dream   He thought of surprising her with a bouquet of flowers. Disheveled flamboyant peach-colored roses and double red roses. Yellow chrysanthemums and streaked tulips and alstromeria of devotion. He felt, however, he needed a reason, first of all for knowing she lived on a mesa near the sea, and secondly, for sending her flowers.

prayer   What to do about these nervous, broken men?

dream   Not so much a night of flowers, but the thought of sending them. How, in a dream, his name was alginate or arginine. How he desired to share her crazed radiant fecklessness. He wrote down the isolated word, bifurcate. No roses reviewed, no water arteries scissored, no streaked tulips. No one ever witnessed his thoughts. Where lay the evidence, except in his hand without a single blossom.

letter   To a woman. Signed, anonymous.

dream   In real life, she received the flowers and assumed, who else?

prayer   *Be perfect as I am perfect.* Innocence in parenthesis.

. . .

Sadness is a thin letter

Received over and over

Once a month

Saying rain or clouded expression

Comes with thin mosquitoes

Waved away, almost inhaled

Insects breeding in water

You put it away in a drawer

A folded shadow touches you

Until the next letter and the next

Self-eclipsing spirit of sorrow

The blind woman says, why not burn it

Love is what makes life-blood sweet

Intrepid forest sings wisdom, afterlife

Love is what dispels blindness

With love there is no fretted screen

Made for viewing grief, only paper

No fretted shoji for snow-viewing

In a dream you are a three-word card

I love you I love you I love

Three times three times three

Taller than a woman yesterday

Who doesn't read such letters

Or a three-toed rhea, feathered

Down under, Australia

Humor me, she says

Long dark nape over her

Avian heart, fused wishbone

Clavicle and flightless wings

I love you I love

Happiness herself

A rare bird

Translated

Ardor

. . .

dream   What did we learn from this story of the pomegranate? They burned the leaves, meaning a violent chorus of humming envy, dislike. The pomegranate's pages flamed, talented dictionary. Comes from not knowing the Holy Spirit as a person, says the blind woman. You are among them but they don't know what to do with you. Try to put you away. Unlabeled box. Lost fruit bowl. God didn't open the door. A few more years, perhaps. A pomegranate's leaves burned the same time you were flowering on the mesa. Other species were embedded in you; jasmines and orange blossoms sprouted from your seeded corneas without the cessation of soil, wheel of incandescence, wheel of dunamos and love.

letter   All the names were written.

prayer   Perhaps burning does stimulate germination.

. . .

In the ladies circle

White women said

You would have been

A good house slave

Because you can stitch

She owned that property

On this and such avenue

Burned to the ground

A white woman

In the ladies circle

Everyone knew how to stitch

White women, prejudiced

Slave with fine hands

I did the stamp collection for them

When I could still see, parting one

From same, their bleached faces

In profile, intaglio, cameo

Placed each one in books

Albums with little pockets

Never understood why

White women

So often photographed

Used bleaching cream

Hydroquinone

Isn't white

White enough

. . .

dream   Went to sea at fourteen searching for the rarities from polar philatelists. Sending a postcard from so far up north or down under. This was a dream. I never went to sea, never witnessed the aurora borealis, magnetic dance of light shaped by solar wind. Never saw the transmission of letters by air, grace of the aerophilately, once airplanes, prayed into existence. What is imagined is made real in dream as a watermark or subtle perforation.

. . .

Cryosurgery

Is not a fine way

To get inside me

Burning red flowers

Growing inside, alive

Said to feel no pain

That was untrue

If flowers could speak

These red flowers shouted

It was very painful, remember

One flower each on the end

Of long individual needles

Little red-brown scabs

Freezing off, burning

Inside a slender anthophore's

Opening, this pomegranate's

Vocal throat silenced in

Sequenced red ellipses . . .

Prayer is seamless

It is water

Goes beneath the literal

Surface of things

Underneath is

Love and order

Ardor

. . .

dream   Light underneath a bushel. Tabled love. Astringency is the beauty of pomegranates, instinctual hiddenness. Persevering under scarlet. Vermilion. The pomegranate is also a lamp, each seed shedding light. And here's what a pomegranate believes. Mineral salts, unwitnessed relinquishment, quotidian grace such as rain and leaf and the gradual strengthening of bone.

prayer   *Vessel of wood or raiment or skin or sack, whatsoever it be, wherein any work is done, it must be put into water, and it shall be unclean until the even; so it shall be cleansed. And every earthen vessel wherein any of them falleth, whatsoever is in it shall be unclean; and ye shall break it.*

letter   Unclean not only from my race but due to blindness. Quarantined for life. Silence except for the leper's cry of unclean, unclean through the scarf. Yet my skin is as the vineyard beloved's in the song of songs. Gold beaten out of unrefined oil. Say *jin* is wellspring *jin* is gold.

    . . .

    Gier eagle? Osprey?

    Bone-breaking birds.

    Why is the cuckoo listed?

    This translation says gull.

    Hoopoe, night hawk, coney.

    Scavengers of flesh.

    Stork, heron, lapwing.

    Plover and shore birds.

    Sandpiper. . . .

    What's left in Leviticus?

    Certain fish species.

    Those with fins and scales.

    Katydids and crickets.

    And grasshoppers.

    All those are clean.

    . . .

letter   On the subject of cleanliness, for instance. Bathe in salt water or diluted vinegar, a shallow sitz bath with iodine. Care for the body's spaces. No odor. Put on fresh clothes and wash all the sheets, linen, bedding, and air out the room unless it's the time of bleeding, especially in winter.

. . .

Prayer is

Wing loading

Proportion, for instance

Bird with a large wing

To a light body

Goes farther

Naming bones

Ulna and radius

Inside the bird's arm

One on each side

Inner and outer

Balance

Long slender bone

Columella

Of the middle ear

Where three

Exist for us

Lastly

Alula

Hardly bone

At all

                          . . .

dream   The word, diurnal. Green chemises.

prayer   Word open, a red geode. Where?

dream   Stone skin, blood within. Love.

                          . . .

             You look darker than usual

             Said a white woman offhand

             Call her white in parenthesis

             Wilted magnolia inside her mouth

             Inverted proposition, dark

             We tan, too, I said, brown-hued

             With a gold pin, ounced amber

             In pairs, hairpins and skin

             Sienna chestnut auburn indio

             Or terra cotta walnut bisque

             Mahogany torso encircled

             Burned red around

             Sliced pound cake

             This ounce of gold

             Rubbed velvet all over skin

             Balm burning inner parts

             Menthol mixed with cassia

             Yet my favorite is a dream

Where I was fully dark blue

Navy blue satin sheets

Yards and yards and yards

Wrapped around this body

So close to nerve unaware

Unreined skin

I was strong as midnight

Where morning waits

Oil lamp of the world

Sleeping there, blue

With a blind woman's poem

Rising a blue roan fish

Scaling the marine dark

With its own oil lamp

Or hinged reading light

Casting words in all hues

Calligraphic indigo

Within skin

. . .

letter   A hidden seam.

. . .

Says the apostle

My heart is enlarged

Unto you

This oil from south Asia

To cure your aphonia

Heal your atrial flutter

Arrhythmia

Place your hand over this heart

Dual butterfly with four hands

Four wings, fibrillation

This chambered heart enlarged

Lush scarlet since new rains

In line for new quarters

Looking for a face to appear

On the circumference of a circle

The blind woman touches a coin

It doesn't look like a whole face

Only a partial surface, transparent

Mingled with waning maria

Or a set of partial tasting glasses

Pinot cabernet riesling viognier

Shorter and slimmer in progression

Pinot noir for the roundest one

First to last, only a face

Dry spirits for the smallest

All without their necks, stemless

Poverty of light, pupils of eight drops

Where are the faces in bas relief

In line for new quarters

Sun costs only a hundred dollars

With a handwritten note cast down

In exchange for a set of heirloom ware

Dollars for the setting sun

Coins, intaglio

Without stems, without new wine

Offal

No fragrance

Behold, says the woman

This crevice in my heart

Enlarged

Is a canyon of love

Wherein dwell birds

Said to mate for life

Mourning doves

Hornbills

Swans

Red-crowned cranes

Magnified

A hundred times

Your love offering

On a gold replica coin

Fragment of frankincense

Real crystal of myrrh

Known also as tears

Aloe and spices

Where is the rare bird

Rising flame to flame

Anointed

Out of the box

Lettered

From earth

Where even annelids

Of five enchained hearts

Survive

As one, separate

Yet a part

. . .

letter   The word, noxious.

. . .

Healing is

Soundless bells

Of candle warmth

Shouldered

Over the body

Generously sheltered

Blood marrow spleen

Eye stirrup uterine

To bear witness

Pure olive oil beaten

For the light

To cause the lamps

To burn continuously

A word, courage

Desires a certain

Leaning inside

This miracle shadow

Called the Christ

Passing all light

Without obstruction

This candle pours

One mold stronger

Than spoken prayer

Offering the shape

Its own body

Ice floe green

Cassia glow

Cylinder of love

Melting

Remittance

Emitting light

Emerald heat translated

Ice green inner ocean

One who comes after me

The thongs of whose sandals

I am not worthy to untie

Water of life foretold

Of a child reared

On the Mediterranean

Loving the isolation

Olive groves

Bearing witness

To such a large body

Of light

. . .

dream   Diastole, opening or dilation of the heart. Systole, pushing blood into the outer regions. Cradle of flesh, core of fellowship therein. What emerges from the body as silk enters in as rain sung sotto. *Yu* for rain *yu* for fish and *yu* in the way of perfume. *Yu xiang.* Not entering with long needles for burning, not even with arthrodia, gliding joints in tarsal articulations. Grotto of healing red tears. Read this blooming mauve and scarlet without the memory of rheumatism.

letter   Sutura vera or true: Of the body's indented articulations.

prayer	Coronary for anything related to the heart, even a milk thistle garden.

    . . .

    Source called Q

    In the synoptic gospels

    L was the original source

    Q had verses common

    To one pair but not

    The other, and not

    The fourth one

    Originality, length

    Degree of reverence

    Q and L together

    Or perhaps not at all

    Only L

    Or maybe Z

    . . .

dream	Ownership sealed by the Holy Spirit.
prayer	Sealed to this arm, gold insignia.
letter	All the lettered alphabetical signs, alpha to omega.

    . . .

    Voice on the other end of the line

    Asking and asking for Aida, Aida

    It's a wrong number, I say

In the background

Another woman's low voice spelling

Anthuriums, perhaps, or

Philodendron

Winter isn't long enough

It should go from

November to November

Full of pomelos, kumquats

It would be cold, rainy, sweet

A little clearing here and there

Quiet as wet macadamia nut shells

Heaped with soft dirt and cinder

Then I would have peace

I would be silent

My anthuriums would thrive

In pots of draining soil

Winter has only

A vase life lasting two months

Like anthuriums

Pressed underwater

Or the entire flower's

Rehydration from the root

Away from heat, drafts

Misted daily

Anthos

Oura

. . .

letter   On a red spathe resembling a petal, sparse postal markings.

dream   Numerical indicia, red-inked comments, index of love.

. . .

Coronal view of winter and shining teeming fishes.

Versus sagittal light, new fins and scales.

If it were winter all year long, what would we do?

Pomelos would be in season all year.

November to March.

What about blood oranges?

December to April.

Kumquats?

. . .

Q for spring-like clarity

Fairness in love, war

Q for *qin* or *ch'ing*

With a water radical

Or human root

Q for quinoa

Q for quassia

Q for quasipublic

Q = qoph

Q for quantify

Q for quell

Q for quickfiring

Q = quantum mechanics

Q for quarantine

Q for quixotic

Q = quotient ring

Q = et cetera

Q = *pi pa*

Who is Q?

What is it?

Stringed *pi pa*

Cusped epicycloid

Your acoustical imagination

. . .

prayer   Used boxes for moving, a blue chess piece now lost, colored fish bred in rainwater, red annelids for composting, two million in cold cash overseas, someone to paint a room the shade of her mother's eyes, one quivering rainforest anywhere in the world, and lots of broken musical instruments.

letter   A loop in the woman's signature, robin's breast red.

dream   Last word, paraphernalia.

. . .

Corn-silk tea to draw excess water out of

This remaining body part, modified apocrine

Lover of blood oranges, flesh streaked red

Opening to the rest of the year and

A voice on the other end imploring

Por favor imprimo numero uno

Question: Winter isn't long enough

Transfigured voice of emotion

Inside a sea wall moaning nightly

Stillness of eye pressure seen

Lifting in fair weather

A coronal view of winter

Versus sagittal light

Or a mirador

Looking

Especially far

. . .

dream   A word, beta-fructofuranosidase.

letter   One drenched with wild honey.

. . .

Between the dry rains

When the acacia and red pepper tree

Were one, neither bearing red fruit

Nor shedding children in arid winds

Prelude to winter's cayenne spice, loosed

The original gardener returned in January

Rain's seasonal pittance misting the fire hills

Lately before the spring deluge

With a generous copper-colored hand

This man took a gold envelope of fire wind

Out of his heart, vascular unbreathing

Old potato, old potato, he mused

Regretting a passed youth, coveting those letters

Of curled cinnamon bark, torsos of thin air

Nervous, broken man: What to do about him?

Slippery gold seal inside his coat's lapel

Ventricles opened to worship, naves of love

One pomegranate embedded with lost progeny

He took a gold envelope from heart's remorse

Opened to a single line, *I envy not the yellow dusk*

You are my book salvaged from spring rain

Following you to the ends of this earth

You've never fallen in love, my dear

Parabola of light over your face

Upper half open in parenthesis

Or do I mean to say ardor in

A woman's long automobile of love

A circle rolling around an . . .

Original gardener

I will follow you to the ends

Turning this ignoble nocturnal heat

Of green lane dispersing late tule remember

Those things once longed for in youth

Flesh pots of petaled quail, cucumbers

A pinch of cumin heated in oil

Even marriage, after marriage

And manna, the abundance

Of God wedded to flesh

Jesus, Son of God

Who is the Christ

Ye su ji du, yes

Tasting wafers

Made with honey

Miracle gift

To a desert exile

Bathed in light

I will follow

My love to

The ends of

This

. . .

dream   Sequence of tangents.

letter   Circumstantial events.

prayer   The blind woman's fragments. I = II = III

. . .

A little agitated, though

Slower than andante

Adagio un poco mosso

Resistance or slight frisson

Of indifference, moss-colored

Falling through a lit spectacle, forest

Of purses, alleluias

Touching one place

Your finger on this body

Tracing one locale

A linear universe forever

Tangible infinity

Helps to remember

When the answer brings

This phrase, not yet

Or still waiting

Women say

All women know when

Someone is falling in love

Women also say women

Never see, purblind to love

Immune to corporeal reality

If love is physical reality

In parenthesis or

Remember the disciple

Who wrote this in a letter

Perfect love drives out fear

Elopement, is it

Without impunity

. . .

Hypothesis

This logarithm of

Love raised to its base

In lowercase italics

Exponential legacy

Of power

. . .

Beating the desire, she says

Beating down the sweltering gold pulse

Bludgeoning a live fish, vibrant sacrifice

Voice of a bleeding perfumery

Fragrance lingering *yu xiang*

In parenthesis not fish, the other *yu*

You know it is personal discipline

Rutilant inside your invisible ruby

Fish flopping over on a chopping block

Unwed liver in the other room, left dished

Not liver you say, the word for lover

You look away from the sacrifice

Or put the desire in a porcelain jar

Odorless, soundless prime

Stored up high on the top shelf

Like a young girl's upturned head

Her mother's kisses transposed in a dream

To mosquitoes kissing the cold surface

Bath water drawn cold, forgotten in the hour

One person, this young girl's irrigated grace

Not the daughter, that is, the childhood

Old weathered points of rain and blood

Mingled in one proboscis of love

. . .

letter   Your own vocabulary of fragrance: Arched beveled rosewood.

. . .

A woman, her mother, said

If you dare fall in love with the wrong man

I'll cut the heart out of your body

You hear me you see you understand

Never fall in love with the wrong man

The young girl's upturned head

Looked around the room for her heart

Which surreptitiously opened the window

Escaped into a hoarse unblinking night

On dark blue match stick legs, navy

Rather than succumb to such a fate

Why navy, she wondered in parenthesis

Has anyone seen a heart my running

Delinquent heart running unsheathed

Pericardium shedding a torn train

Platelets for clotting, enucleated cells

Streetlight to streetlight, stemless glass

Stranded emerald mauve rope breathing

Hand-twisted, lowered into wilderness

Eloping blindly with the unknown

Is love alluvial

Novel to this universe

I lay myself down, shot through

Who am I without my . . .

Is it running toward

To grope without name or body

Not even a teetering pail of red paint

To acquire a new surface, anonymous

On the signature line, X or Z

Was it vaudeville or opera

The heart sang while choking inside

Arduous fields of showering green

Circuits pulsing, crushed, glittering

Resurrected oar of love

Slipping in water

Let's go away, elope

To where

Love

Her mother, the woman

Warned her about the drift

As brass or was it

Pian xing, literal drift

Upstream or subtle place

A little far to the left or right

Subtle perforation

Unreliable human

Instinctual boundaries

An imaginary box, her pulse

Lifting a closed night window

Years later, not looking back

Dying to the self

In doing so, a red poppy blooms

Absence of a calendar page

Jar the lost heart now lives in

Universe

Drifting abroad with red wings

Heralding pure emerald

I walked up ninety steps today

Sat in the first car of the train

Broken escalator at the far end

Prompt for the absent heart

To receive aerobic exercise

Calisthenics

Modulation as meaning drifts

In one translation to another

Modest form of radical love

Or remembrance holding together

Calque alphabet

This swift untied suitcase

How the original gardener

With one raised hand

Bleeding nail burns, cayenne

Returns at the moment

You least expect

Recurrence

To see

Ascending and arching

Gliding

In unbroken glory

Mourning doves

Hornbills

Swans

Red-crowned cranes

Spirit married

To flesh

Streaming

Out of sun

Ardor

. . .

letter   The women's auxiliary.

dream   Call at one o'clock. Work on the prayer requests then.

. . .

Pentecostal

Gesture of regeneration

In the biblical quest for a new heart

Lightness the infallible object

Slain in the Spirit, trembling

Desuetude without wind

Persuasion, the Spirit's silent work

Pray to send the gifts of healing

Impulse should dwell in the we

One accord

Never use the word, delirium

Delphinium?

She took the pomegranate and put it up high

Safe in the closet from prying eyes

Gold-leaf wings, ventricles

Pulsing above books

Beautiful uterine heart

Sits as a fiery regal bird

Without whistles, clicks, murmurs

Fruit of a hundred thousand preconceived

Embedded blossoms, each red-bronze pearl

One blossom invested within

Remember

God became a man

This inner room without strife

Poured out cleansing blood

This inner arm, one lotus

This torso, this temple

Four arenas of thunder

Chrysanthemum

Rose of the world

Fringe-limbed

Pierced

Golden

Blue-sided

Son

. . .

dream   Hard finding one another to love within an endangered species.

letter   Please pray for the kwashiorkor, famished red boy.

prayer   Of late, the dry rains, hard as barley seed, grieve our crop. Please pray for a merciful softening of rains. Try to remember what we originally wrote. Should we ask for a fresh anointing to pray with boldness for traveling mercies? How should we pray for recurrent rains? Look at material shimmering underneath the hand, moving before the eye can glimpse the weave. Read to the fourth line today, and if you can, the seventh line. Much sorrow eclipsed for the healing to pass through an optic nerve, or not enough love, dunamos of the holy wind, not yet.

letter   Promised long before the healing envelope of deliverance is received.

. . .

Any of your close kin

With high blood pressure

Tuberculosis

Rheumatic heart

Congenital heart

None of the above

What is congenital heart

A failure or condition?

Since we all have hearts at birth

Is that congenital

Do you regularly smoke

Or drink bottles of wine

No

Do you take iron

Or blood medications

Sleeping pills

None of the above

Once I had crushed foxglove leaves

Digitalis

Was it bittersweet?

Cardiac stimulant and diuretic

Finger-shaped corolla

Love story rolled in a kola nut

Strong as the petaled firmament's

Longitudinal transference

To a form of grace laying

Phloem rods of light

Purses of august favor

Red-laced and gold-laced

Alleviating wing pressure

On optic nerves

Olive groves

Orchards of spiced wine

Fig cakes pressed

In your arduous daily labor

I persist

. . .

dream   How champagne flute glasses sold at a hundred dollars
         relate to the elephant sanctuary.

letter   The word, aventurine. Red adventure or marine on a
          brass ring.

prayer   If you purchase one of these flute glasses, a percentage
          contribution will be made in your name to the
          elephant sanctuary. Or you may choose to remain
          anonymous.

dream   One of the elephants is in need of cataract surgery.
         She is blind, although her infant daughter is sighted in
         both eyes. The infant follows her mother to the water
         trees where she stands underneath the blind matriarch
         for shade and protection, though no predators live in
         the sanctuary.

         . . .

         I shut the door against callers

         To write a poem

         Swallows and caked fragrance

Fill my thoughts

In solitude, I find companions

In form of birds and imaginary men

She too is fond of putting herself

In parenthesis, *tracing a curve*

Six volumes of *ci* or *tz'u*, lyrics

Seven volumes of *shi* or poetry

Gathered fruit, charcoal rubbings

Various inscriptions

Collected antiquities

Her husband's work titled

Records on metal and stone

They adored collecting art

Most of their possessions burned

Only five to seven baskets remained

Calligraphy, paintings, ink stones

In hindsight, I return to the small

Cycles of loss and gain

We indicated flaws or errata

One burning candle dimmed

How does a Song dynasty poet

Relate to this Western

Female poet of Asian lineage

Sparce winds fills the blinds

With a fragrance of roses

How am I kin to a woman

Li Qingzhao or Li Ch'ing-chao

Whose surname

Brings mine to light

In this language

The long-hidden sonnet

A lee of water potential

Slips from an open sleeve

With a couplet in parenthesis:

An avian or potential beauty

Matures the living water for a duration:

A gift of quiet potential purity

At equal ambiance and assignation.

As dormancy in spaces of potential

Flows in places lower than the sea,

Water seems more secret than prudential

When described in terms of transparency.

As aqueous potential in solution,

Density of faith under chloroform

And sleep of faculties, precipitation

Increases pressure on poetic form.

(A rainbird crying in a water drain

is commonly believed to augur rain.)

. . .

prayer   Another place without predators is *tan tien*. Heaven.

letter   Cardioid ardor in parenthesis or avian sonnet in
         rhymed quatrains.

dream   All the unclean birds granted immunity from
         quarantine.

         . . .

         Pray that pressures remain eight and eight

         In the left and right eyes, water potential

         As a form of intraocular lightening

         In the utterance of one woman's vision

         Resisting closed form

         No known tongues contain this

         Heart-shaped curve . . .

         You pray things into existence

         Realities of hindsight are considered

         For things that haven't occurred yet

         Voicing the evidence of faith, a priori

         Prayer: The sky is four hundred boats

         Filled with yellow chrysanthemums

         Overturned when the saints are sleeping

         Dream: A woman opens her eyes

         Letter: When it rains *xia yu*

         You see the curious way of stones in a river

         Kwashiorkor, red boy of famine, thirsts

How a hand wears down or lifts

Obstacles to miraculous recovery, antidote

Restores fruit-bearing life, two lemon trees

Dioecious in dry rains, male and female

Lime trees without blossoms for years

Carried on separate bodies, linen

Staminate and pistillate flowers

Burning down, burning over

Passing through the furnace

Your eyes shot through, unconditionally burned

Bound in the Holy Ghost, caught up over

To the third heaven: *My ears had heard of you*

But now my eyes have seen you

Setting bones, an unseen surgeon

Cures the inconstant vision

Delineates hidden shapes

Pressuring love at first

Plunging deeper than

The first optic rain

You in parenthesis raining

Over retinal insight

Amen

. . .

notes

Epigraphs:
>*The word is near you* . . . (NIV Romans 10:8)
>*Faith is that quality or power* . . . (Kuhlman 200)
>*It is hard to describe* . . . (from "*Man ting fang:* A fragrant courtyard" by Li Qingzhao)

A heart-shaped curve traced by a point . . . (Merriam-Webster, p. 207)

Vessel of wood or raiment or skin or sack . . . (KJ Leviticus 11:32–33)

Pure olive oil beaten . . . (KJ Leviticus 24:2)

One who comes after me . . . (NIV John 1:27)

Perfect love drives out fear (NIV 1 John 4:18)

Finger-shaped corolla (Merriam-Webster 354)

My ears had heard of you . . . (KJ Job 42:65)

Gray's Anatomy and Freethy's *How Birds Work* provided valuable information about human and avian anatomies. Additionally, the following are excerpts from my translations of Li Qingzhao's poetry and prose (Song Dynasty, 1084 – ca. 1151).

We shared fresh tea, the fire of life . . . ("*Xiao meng:* Sunrise dream")

High spirits waned as our boat turned late . . . ("*Ru meng ling:* As if a reverie")

A man offered to sell us a painting of peonies by Xu Xi . . . ("*Jin shi lu hou xu:* Records on metal and stone, epilogue")

Books . . . a commissioned string of connected boats . . .

("*Jin shi lu hou xu:* Records on metal and stone, epilogue")

I envy not the yellow dusk . . . ("*Qing qing chao man:* Celebrating a slow luminous dawn")

I shut the door against callers . . . ("Gan huai shi: Poem of emotions")

All that remained were six or so baskets . . . ("*Jin shi lu hou xu:* Records on metal and stone, epilogue")

Sparse wind fills the blinds . . . ("*Chun chan:* Spring fades")

sources

Freethy, Ron. *How Birds Work: A Guide to Bird Biology.* New York: Blandford Press, 1982.

Gray, Henry. *Gray's Anatomy.* Edited by T. Pickering Pick and Robert Howden, New York: Crown Publishers, 1977.

The Holy Bible: Old and New Testaments in the King James Version. Giant Print Edition. Nashville, Tennessee: Regency Publishing House, 1973.

The Holy Bible: New International Version. Grand Rapids, Michigan: Zondervan Publishing House, 1984.

"Li Qingzhao." Ming-Qing Women's Writings Digitization Project. Yenching Library, Harvard University. 2005. <http://digital.library.mcgill.ca/mingqing/english/index.htm>

Webster's Ninth New Collegiate Dictionary. Springfield, MA: Merriam-Webster Inc., Publishers, 1985.